THE BOOK OF BEST

SPORTS QUOTES

FUNNY, INSPIRATIONAL AND MOTIVATIONAL QUOTES ON THE SPORTS WE LOVE

By M. Prefontaine

https://twitter.com/quotes4livingby

https://www.facebook.com/QuotesForLivingby/

INTRODUCTION

This is a book for those who love sport and all that goes with it. Most of us have played sports where people have said something amusing, inspirational or just exquisitely stupid. It is a part of the enjoyment of sports and those experiences are shared with team mates and competitors.

This collection of quotes which I have assembled here is essentially the similar experiences of the great and the good of their respective sports.

Table of Contents

Chapter 1. General

Sports are the reason I am out of shape. I watch them all on TV.
-Thomas Sowell (1930 -)

You meet a better class of person at the back of the grid.
-Graham Hill (1929 – 75)

I've learned that something constructive comes from every defeat.
–Tom Landry (1924 – 2000)

Winners aren't born, they are made.
-Matthew Syed (1970 -)

It's okay to get knocked down. What happens next says it all.
-Rick Macci

So when you participate in sporting events, it's not whether you win or lose. It's how drunk you get.
-Homer Simpson/Dan Castellaneta

Practice isn't the thing you do once you're good. It's the thing you do that makes you good.
-Malcolm Gladwell (1963 -)

The only way to prove that you're a good sport is to lose.
–Ernie Banks (1931 – 2015)

If the bible has taught us nothing, and it hasn't, it's that girls should stick to girls' sports, such as hot oil wrestling, foxy boxing and such and such.
-Homer Simpson/Dan Castellaneta

Only he who can see the invisible can do the impossible.
–Frank L. Gaines (1921 – 2012)

When you're riding, only the race in which you're riding is important.
– Bill Shoemaker (1931 – 2003)

Age is no barrier. It's a limitation you put on your mind.
-Jackie Joyner-Kersee (1962 -)

I always felt that my greatest asset was not my physical ability, it was my mental ability.
–Bruce Jenner (1949 -)

A trophy carries dust. Memories last forever.
–Mary Lou Retton (1968 -)

Most people give up just when they're about to achieve success. They quit on the one yard line. They give up at the last minute of the game one foot from a winning touchdown.
–Ross Perot (1930 -)

You have to do something in your life that is honorable and not cowardly if you are to live in peace with yourself.
–Larry Brown (1940 -)

The five S's of sports training are: stamina, speed, strength, skill, and spirit; but the greatest of these is spirit.
–Ken Doherty (1969 -)

An athlete cannot run with money in his pockets. He must run with hope in his heart and dreams in his head.
-Emil Zatopek (1922 – 2000)

Somewhere behind the athlete you've become and the hours of practice and the coaches who have pushed you is a little girl who fell in love with the game and never looked back... play for her.
-Mia Hamm (1972 -)

When you've got something to prove, there's nothing greater than a challenge.
–Terry Bradshaw (1948 -)

Never give up, never give in, and when the upper hand is ours, may we have the ability to handle the win with the dignity that we absorbed the loss.
–Doug Williams (1955 -)

Most people never run far enough on their first wind to find out they've got a second.
-William James (1842 – 1910)

The difference between the impossible and the possible lies in a person's determination.
-Tommy Lasorda (1927 -)

Sports serve society by providing vivid examples of excellence.
–George F. Will (1941 -)

The more difficult the victory, the greater the happiness in winning.
–Pele (1940 -)

The mind is the limit. As long as the mind can envision the fact that you can do something, you can do it, as long as you really believe 100 percent.
–Arnold Schwarzenegger (1947 -)

I always turn to the sports section first. The sports page records people's accomplishments; the front page has nothing but man's failures.
-Earl Warren (1891 – 1974)

Every sport pretends to a literature, but people don't believe it of any other sport but their own.
-Alistair Cooke (1908 – 2004)

The difference between the old ballplayer and the new ballplayer is the jersey. The old ballplayer cared about the name on the front. The new ballplayer cares about the name on the back.
-Steve Garvey (1948 -)

When we played, World Series checks meant something. Now all they do is screw up your taxes.
-Don Drysdale (1936 – 93)

Prize fighters can sometimes read and write when they start — but they can't when they finish.

-Martin H. Fischer (1879 – 1962)

One day of practice is like one day of clean living. It doesn't do you any good.

-Abe Lemmons (1922 – 2002)

The more you sweat in practice, the less you bleed in battle.

-Anon

I wanted to have a career in sports when I was young, but I had to give it up. I'm only six feet tall, so I couldn't play basketball. I'm only 190 pounds, so I couldn't play football. And I have 20-20 vision, so I couldn't be a referee.

-Jay Leno (1950 -)

It is all very well to say that a man should play for the pure love of the game. Perhaps he ought, but to the working man it is impossible.

-JJ Bentley

I know we're meant to be these hard-headed, money-obsessed professionals but we're still little boys at heart. Just ask our wives.

-Rob Lee (1966 -)

As a manager, you always have a gun to your head. It's a question of whether there is a bullet in the barrel.

-Kevin Keegan (1951 -)

The breakfast of champions is not cereal, it's the opposition.
-Nick Seitz

We are inclined that if we watch a football game or baseball game, we have taken part in it.
-John F. Kennedy (1917 – 63)

The umpire... is like the geyser in the bathroom; we cannot do without it, yet we notice it only when it is out of order.
-Neville Cardus (1888 – 1975)

There isn't a single professional sports season now that doesn't go on at least a month too long. Baseball starts in football weather, and football in baseball weather, and basketball overlaps them both.
-James Reston (1909 – 95)

Officials are the only guys who can rob you and then get a police escort out of the stadium.
-Ron Bolton (1950 -)

I was called "Rembrandt" Hope in my boxing days, because I spent so much time on the canvas.
-Bob Hope (1903 – 2003)

To dope the racer is as criminal, as sacrilegious, as trying to imitate God; it is stealing from God the privilege of the spark.
-Roland Barthes (1915 – 80)

Losing streaks are funny. If you lose at the beginning, you get off to a bad start. If you lose in the middle of the season, you're in a slump. If you lose at the end, you're choking.
-Gene Mauch (1925 – 2005)

People understand contests. You take a bunch of kids throwing rocks at random and people look askance, but if you go and hold a rock-throwing contest — people understand that.
-Don Murray (1929 -)

When it comes to sports I am not particularly interested. Generally speaking, I look upon them as dangerous and tiring activities performed by people with whom I share nothing except the right to trial by jury.
-Fran Lebowitz (1950 -)

I cannot for the life of me see why the umpires, the only two people on a cricket field who are not going to get grass stains on their knees, are the only two people allowed to wear dark trousers.
-Katharine Whitehorn (1928 -)

Cricket — a game which the English, not being a spiritual people, have invented in order to give themselves some conception of eternity.
-Lord Mancroft (1957 -)

Oh God, if there be cricket in heaven, let there also be rain.
-Alec Douglas Home (1903 – 95)

Left hand, right hand, it doesn't matter. I'm amphibious.
–*Charles Shackleford (1966 -)*

The drivers have one foot on the brake, one on the clutch, and one on the throttle.
-Bob Varsha (1951 -)

CHAPTER 2 AMERICAN FOOTBALL

If it doesn't matter who wins or loses, then why do they keep score?
-Vince Lombardi (1913 – 70)

If defensive linemen's IQs were 5 points lower, they'd be geraniums.
-Russ Francis (1953 -)

Football is a game for trained apes.
Edward Abbey (1927 – 89)

Perfection is not attainable. But if we chase perfection, we can catch excellence.
-Vince Lombardi (1913 – 70)

Losing the Super Bowl is worse than death. With death you don't have to get up in the morning.
-George Allen (1918 – 90)

Leadership is a matter of having people look at you and gain confidence...If you're in control, they're in control.
-Tom Landry (1924 – 2000)

American Football is Rugby after a visit from the Health and Safety Inspector.
- Anon

If you want to win, do the ordinary things better than anyone else does them day in and day out.
-Chuck Noll (1932 – 2014)

Leaders are made, they are not born. They are made by hard effort, which is the price which all of us must pay to achieve any goal that is worthwhile.
-Vince Lombardi (1913 – 70)

I wouldn't ever set out to hurt someone deliberately unless it was, you know, important – like a league game.
-Dick Butkus (1942 -)

You fail all the time, but you aren't a failure until you start blaming someone else.
-Bum Phillips (1923 – 2013)

Football is not a contact sport; it is a collision sport. Dancing is a contact sport.
-Duffy Daugherty (1915 – 87)

Success demands singleness of purpose.
-Vince Lombardi (1913 – 70)

Physically he is a world beater. Mentally he's an egg beater.
-Matt Elliot (1968 -)

Nobody who ever gave his best regretted it.
-George S. Halas (1895 – 1983)

I'll tell you, there were only a few games in my career where I was totally oblivious to everything around me, where I was in the zone.
-Lawrence Taylor (1985 -)

On this team we were all united on a common goal; to keep my job.
-Lou Holtz (1937 -)

Fear can be conquered. I became a better person and a better football player when I learned that lesson.
-Roger Craig (1960 -)

College football is a sport that bears the same relation to education that bullfighting does to agriculture.
-Elbert Hubbard (1856 – 1915)

Pressure is something you feel when you don't know what the hell you're doing.
-Peyton Manning (1976 -)

Make sure when anyone tackles you he remembers how much it hurts.
-Jim Brown (1936 -)

I feel like I'm the best, but you're not going to get me to say that.
-Jerry Rice (1962 -)

There is a difference between conceit and confidence. Conceit is bragging about yourself. Confidence means you believe you can get the job done.
-Johnny Unitas (1933 – 2002)

I looked in the mirror one day and I said to my wife 'How many great coaches do uou think there are?' She said ' One less than you think.'
-Joe Paterno (1926 – 2012)

If my mother put on a helmet and shoulder pads and a uniform that wasn't the same as the one I was wearing, I'd run over her if she was in my way. And I love my mother.
-Bo Jackson (1962 -)

Gary Anderson is a great player. He ceases to amaze me every day.
-Ray Perkins (1941 -)

You have to play this game like somebody just hit your mother with a two-by-four.
-Dan Birdwell (1940 – 78)

I have found that prayers work best when you have big players.
-Knute Rockne (188 – 1931)

It's not the size of the dog in the fight, but the size of the fight in the dog.
-Archie Griffin (1954 -)

If we didn't have a huddle, Jim (Burt) would have no social life.
-*Phil Simms (1954 -)*

Ability is what you're capable of doing. Motivation determines what you do. Attitude determines how well you do it.
-*Lou Holtz (1937 -)*

We've got Keeney on the lettuce diet. Unfortunately, he eats 40 pounds of lettuce a day.
-*Steve Sloan (1944 -)*

I firmly believe that any man's finest hour, the greatest fulfillment of all that he holds dear, is the moment when he has worked his heart out in a good cause and lies exhausted on the field of battle-victorious.
-*Vince Lombardi (1913 – 70)*

I never really lost a game in my career, sometimes I just ran out of time.
-*Bobby Layne (1926 – 86)*

I like to believe that my best hits border on felonious assault.
-*Jack Tatum (1948 – 2010)*

Football is like life, it requires perseverance, self-denial, hard work sacrifice, dedication and respect for authority.
-*Vince Lombardi (1913 – 70)*

Leaders aren't born, they are made. And they are made just like anything else, through hard work. And that's the price we'll have to pay to achieve that goal, or any goal.
-Vince Lombardi (1913 – 70)

If you aren't going all the way, why go at all?
-Joe Namath (1943 -)

I can't believe that God put us on this earth to be ordinary.
-Lou Holtz (1937 -)

There is a difference in being in shape and being in football shape. Anyone can out on the field and run around , but once you start getting hit and have to get up then you find out the difference between being in shape and football shape.
-John Madden (1936 -)

No one has ever drowned in sweat.
-Lou Holtz (1937 -)

Show me a good loser, and I'll show you a loser.
-Vince Lombardi (1913 – 70)

The man who complains about the way the ball bounces is likely the one who dropped it.
-Lou Holtz (1937 -)

It is essential to understand that battles are primarily won in the hearts of men.
-Vince Lombardi (1913 – 70)

Obstacles are what you see when you take your eyes off the goal.
-*Vince Lombardi (1913 – 70)*

It's a better view if you're standing up than if you're laying down.
-*Lou Holtz (1937 -)*

The reason women don't play football is because eleven of them would never wear the same outfit in public.
-*Phyllis Diller (1917 – 2012)*

I just wrap my arms around the whole backfield and peel'em one by one until I get to the ball carrier. Him, I keep.
-*Eugene Lipscomb (1931 – 1963)*

Most football players are temperamental. That's 90 percent temper and 10 percent mental.
-*Doug Plank (1953 -)*

Rapport? You mean like, you run as fast as you can, and I'll throw it as far as I can?
-*Jeff Kemp (1959 -)*

We're as clean as any team. We wash our hands before we hit anybody.
-*Nate Newton (1961 -)*

I'm a light eater. As soon as it's light, I start to eat.
-*Art Donovan (1924 – 2013)*

You don't have to win it; just don't lose it.
-Ray Lewis (1975 -)

I had pro offers from the Detroit Lions and Green Bay Packers, who were pretty hard up for linemen in those days. If I had gone into professional football the name Jerry Ford might have been a household word today.
-President Gerald Ford (1913 – 2006)

Tom Landry is such a perfectionist that if he were married to Dolly Parton, he'd ask her to cook.
-Don Meredith (1938 – 2010)

He couldn't spell cat if you spotted him the C and the T.
-Thomas Hollywood Henderson (1953 -)

I may be dumb, but I'm not stupid.
-Terry Bradshaw (1948 -)

In Montana, they renamed a town after an all-time great, Joe Montana. Well, a town in Massachusetts changed their name to honor my guy Terry Bradshaw — Marblehead.
-Howie Long (1960 -)

I never graduated college, but I was only there for two terms – Truman's and Eisenhower's.
-Alex Karras (1935 – 2012)

People say I'll be drafted in the first round, maybe even higher.
-Craig Ironhead Heyward (1966 – 2006)

The NFL, like life, is full of idiots.
-Randy Cross (1954 -)

My knees look like they lost a knife fight with a midget.
-E.J. Holub (1938 -)

You're kind of numb after 50 shots to the head.
-Jim Harbaugh (1963 -)

I don't know what he has. A pulled groin. A hip flexor. I don't know. A pulled something. I never pulled anything. You can't pull fat.
-Bruce Coslet (1946 -)

When you win, nothing hurts.
-Joe Namath (1943 -)

Pro football is like nuclear warfare. There are no winners, only survivors.
-Frank Gifford (1930 -2015)

What's one more torpedo in a sinking ship?
-Lynn Dickey (1949 -)

American football makes Rugby look like a Tupperware party.
-Sue Lawley (1946 -)

If you're mad at your kid, you can either raise him to be a nose tackle or send him out to play on the freeway. It's about the same.
-Bob Golic (1957 -)

It is better to give a lick than receive one.
-Bo Jackson (1962 -)

I wouldn't ever set out to hurt anyone deliberately unless it was important – like a league game.
-Dick Butkus (1942 -)

The Bears are so tough when they finish sacking the quarterback, they go after his family in the stands.
-Tim Wrightman (1960 -)

I'd run over my own mother to win the Super Bowl.
-Joe Jacoby (1959 -)

To win, I'd run over Joe's mom, too.
-Matt Millen (1958 -)

We didn't have steroids. If I wanted to get pumped up, I drank a case of beer.
-Art Donovan (1924 – 2013)

When it's third and ten, you can take the milk drinkers, and I'll take the whiskey drinkers every time.
-Max McGee (1932 – 2007)

A good back makes his own holes. Anybody can run where the holes are.
-Joe Don Looney (1942 – 1988)

Baseball is what we were. Football is what we have become.
-Mary McGrory (1918 – 2004)

Maybe a good rule in life is never become too important to do your own laundry.
-Barry Sanders (1968 -)

If a man watches three football games in a row, he should be declared legally dead.
-Erma Bombeck (1927 – 96)

Confidence is a very fragile thing.
-Joe Montana (1956 -)

Confidence doesn't come out of nowhere. It's a result of something - hours and days and weeks and years of constant work and dedication.
-Roger Staubach (1942 -)

There is no defense against a perfect pass. I can throw the perfect pass.
-Dan Marino (1961 -)

I don't know whether I prefer Astroturf to grass. I never smoked Astroturf.
-Joe Namath (1943 -)

In the long run, the cream always rises and the crap always sinks.
-John Elway (1960 -)

I normally run the 40-yard dash in 4.9, but when a 280-pound guy is chasing me, I run it in 4.6.
-John Elway (1960 -)

Now that I'm retired, I want to say that all defensive linemen are sissies.
-Dan Fouts (1951 -)

Sure, the home-field is an advantage — but so is having a lot of talent.
-Dan Marino (1961 -)

If you're a pro coach, NFL stands for not for long.
-Jerry Glanville (1941 -)

Sure, luck means a lot in football. Not having a good quarterback is bad luck.
-Don Shula (1930 -)

If I drop dead tomorrow, at least I'll know I died in good health.
-Bum Phillips (1923 – 2013)

If I didn't enjoy gloating so much, I wouldn't do so many interviews.
-Jimmy Johnson (1943 -)

He can be a great player in this league if he learns how to say two words: I'm full.
-Jerry Glanville (1941 -)

What's the difference between a 3-week-old puppy and a sportswriter? In six weeks, the puppy stops whining.
-Mike Ditka (1939 -)

What's that? Uh — playoffs? Don't talk about — playoffs?!
You kidding me?! Playoffs?! I just hope we can win a game!
-Jim Mora (1935 -)

The only yardstick for success our society has is being a
champion. No one remembers anything else.
-John Madden (1936 -)

Whats the toughest thing in a professional football game?
It's being the mother of the quarterback — toughest thing.
-John Madden (1936 -)

We're not attempting to circumcise rules.
-Bill Cowher (1957 -)

Most of my clichés aren't original.
-Chuck Knox (1932 -)

I'm fairly confident that if I died tomorrow, Don would find a
way to preserve me until the season was over and he had
time for a nice funeral.
-Dorothy Shula (1930 -)

You guys line up alphabetically by height.
-Bill Peterson (1920 – 1993)

We can't run. We can't pass. We can't stop the run. We can't
stop the pass. We can't kick. Other than that, we're just not a
very good football team right now.
-Bruce Coslet (1946 -)

The road to Easy Street goes through the sewer.
-John Madden (1936 -)

Setting a goal is not the main thing. It is deciding how you will go about achieving it and staying with that plan.
-Tom Landry (1924 – 2000)

Men, I want you just thinking of one word all season. One word and one word only: Super Bowl.
-Bill Peterson (1920 – 1993)

The shoulder surgery was a success. The lobotomy failed.
-Mike Ditka (1939 -)

The dictionary is the only place where success comes before work.
-Vince Lombardi (1913 – 70)

It's not whether you get knocked down, it's whether you get up.
-Vince Lombardi (1913 – 70)

Confidence is contagious. So is lack of confidence.
-Vince Lombardi (1913 – 70)

If you aren't fired with enthusiasm, you will be fired with enthusiasm.
-Vince Lombardi (1913 – 70)

Winners never quit, and quitters never win.
-Vince Lombardi (1913 – 70)

Winning isn't everything; it is the only thing.
-Vince Lombardi (1913 – 70)

In great attempts, it is glorious even to fail.
-Vince Lombardi (1913 – 70)

Football combines two of the worst things in American life. It is violence punctuated by committee meetings.
-George Will (1941 -)

CHAPTER 3. BASEBALL

Baseball is like church. Many attend, few understand.
-Leo Durocher (1905 – 91)

I like my players to be married and in debt. That's the way to motivate them.
-Ernie Banks (1931 – 2015)

Baseball has the great advantage over cricket of being sooner ended.
-George Bernard Shaw (1856-1950)

If a tie is like kissing your sister. Losing is like kissing your grandmother with her teeth out.
-George Brett (1953 -)

Any minute, any day, some players may break a long standing record. That's one of the fascinations about the game, the unexpected surprises.
-Cornelius McGillicuddy, Sr. (1862-1956)

How can we keep the Atlanta Braves on their toes ? Raise the urinals.
-Darrel Chaney (1948 -)

Baseball is more than a game to me, it's a religion.
-William Joseph Klem (1874-1951)

Could be that Bill Terry's a nice guy when you get to know him, but why bother?
-Dizzy Dean (1910 – 74)

Poets are like baseball pitchers. Both have their moments. The intervals are the tough things.
-Robert Lee Frost (1874 – 1963)

I never question the integrity of an umpire. Their eyesight, yes.
-Leo Durbocher (1905 – 91)

Every strike brings me closer to the next home run.
-Babe Ruth (1895 – 1948)

The average age of our bench is deceased.
-Tommy Lasorda (1927 -)

I'll convert a school desk into a tricycle, because how else am I supposed to learn to love? It's not like baseball gloves are very effective oven mitts.
-Jarod Kintz (1982 -)

When I was a little boy, I wanted to be a baseball player and join the circus. With the Yankees I have accomplished both.
-Craig Nettles (1944 -)

The thing I write will be the thing I write.
-Steve Shilstone

His limitations are limitless.
-Danny Ozark (1923 – 2009)

My baseball team is called the I Ams. Just me and my clones on the roster. We're devastating. Well, at least I am.
-Jarod Kintz (1982 -)

How can anyone as slow as you pull a muscle?
-Pete Rose (1941-)

It took me seventeen years to get three thousand hits in baseball. It took one afternoon on the golf course.
-Hank Aaron (1934 -)

I'm not a win at all costs guy. Winning isn't everything. It's second to breathing.
-George Steinbrenner (1930 – 2010)

I watch baseball on TV like my cat watches the window. Somebody open the blinds so we can see better!"
-Jarod Kintz (1982 -)

The secret of managing is to keep the guys who hate you away from the guys who are undecided.
-Casey Stengel (1890 – 1975)

Athletes are born winners, there not born loosers, and the sooner you understand this, the faster you can take on a winning attitude and become successful in life.
-Charles R. Sledge Jr. (1957-)

Baseball is the only game left for people. To play basketball you have to be seven foot six. To play football you have to be the same width.
-Bill Veeck (1914 – 86)

No matter how good you are, you're going to lose one-third of your games. No matter how bad you are you're going to win one-third of your games. It's the other third that makes the difference.
-*Tommy Lasorda (1927 -)*

I have discovered in 20 years of moving around a ball park that the knowledge of the game is usually in inverse proportion to the price of the seats.
-*Bill Veeck (1914 – 86)*

A ballplayer spends a good piece of his life gripping a baseball, and in the end it turns out that it was the other way around all the time.
-*Jim Bouton (1939 -)*

Baseball is a game with a lot of waiting in it; it is a game with increasingly heightened anticipation of increasingly limited action.
-*John Irving (1942 -)*

They say some of my stars drink whiskey. But I have found that the ones who drink milkshakes don't win many ball games.
-*Fred McMane*

I do what I've trained my whole life to do. I watch the ball. I keep my eye on the ball. I never stop watching.
I watch it as it sails past me and lands in the catcher's mitt, a perfect and glorious strike three."
-*Barry Lyga (1971 -)*

The sheer quantity of brain power that hurled itself voluntarily and quixotically into the search for new baseball knowledge was either exhilarating or depressing, depending on how you felt about baseball. The same intellectual resources might have cured the common cold, or put a man on Pluto.
-Michael Lewis (1960 -)

Every day is a new opportunity. You can build on yesterday's success or put its failures behind and start over again. That's the way life is, with a new game every day, and that's the way baseball is.
-Bob Feller (1918 – 2010)

There are three types of baseball players: Those who make it happen, those who watch it happen and those who wonder what happens.
-Tommy Lasorda (1927 -)

Baseball was, is and always will be to me the best game in the world.
-Babe Ruth (1895 – 1948)

One of the beautiful things about baseball is that every once in a while you come into a situation where you want to, and where you have to, reach down and prove something.
-Nolan Ryan (1947 -)

God knows I gave my best in baseball at all times and no man on earth can truthfully judge me otherwise.
-Shoeless Joe Jackson (1887 – 1951)

Baseball is the only field of endeavor where a man can succeed three times out of ten and be considered a good performer.
-*Ted Williams (1918 – 2002)*

Opening day. All you have to do is say the words and you feel the shutters thrown wide, the room air out, the light pour in. In baseball, no other day is so pure with possibility. No scores yet, no losses, no blame or disappointment. No hangover, at least until the game's over.
-*Mary Schmich (1953 -)*

Baseball is a lot like life. It's a day-to-day existence, full of ups and downs. You make the most of your opportunities in baseball as you do in life.
-*Ernie Harwell (1918 – 2010)*

Now there's three things you can do in a baseball game: You can win or you can lose or it can rain.
-*Charles Dillon Stengel (1890-1975)*

People ask me what I do in winter when there's no baseball. I'll tell you what I do. I stare out the window and wait for spring.
-*Rogers Hornsby, Sr. (1896-1963)*

My father kept me busy from dawn to dusk when I was a kid. When I wasn't pitching hay, hauling corn or running a tractor, I was heaving a baseball into his mitt behind the barn... If all the parents in the country followed his rule, juvenile delinquency would be cut in half in a year's time.
-*Bob Feller (1918 – 2010)*

Athletes and musicians make astronomical amounts of money. People get paid $100 million to throw a baseball! Shouldn't we all take less and pass some of that money onto others? Think about firefighters, teachers and policemen. We should celebrate people that are intellectually smart and trying to make this world a better place.
-Kid Rock (1971 -)

You can't sit on a lead and run a few plays into the line and just kill the clock. You've got to throw the ball over the damn plate and give the other man his chance. That's why baseball is the greatest game of them all.
-Eurl Weaver (1930 – 2013)

Major league baseball has asked its players to stop tossing baseballs into the stands during games, because they say fans fight over them and they get hurt. In fact, the Florida Marlins said that's why they never hit any home runs. It's a safety issue.
-Jay Leno (1950 -)

Baseball it is said is only a game. True and the Grand Canyon is only a hole in the ground.
-George Will (1941-)

Yogi Berra quotes

I usually take a two-hour nap from one to four.

Never answer an anonymous letter.

I'm not going to buy my kids an encyclopedia. Let them walk to school like I did.

You can observe a lot by watching.

The future ain't what it used to be.

If you don't know where you are going, you might wind up someplace else.

Why buy good luggage, you only use it when you travel.

When you come to a fork in the road, take it.

Nobody goes there anymore, it's too crowded.

It gets late early out here.

I don't know (if they were male or female) fans running naked across the field). They had bags over their heads.

Always go to other people's funerals, otherwise they won't come to yours.

It ain't over 'til it's over.

When you come to a fork in the road take it.

Cut my pie into four pieces, I don't think I could eat eight.

In theory, there is no difference between theory and practice. But in practice, there is.

90% of the game is half mental.

I wish I had an answer to that because I'm tired of answering that question.

Half the lies they tell about me aren't true.

I never said most of the things I said.

If the world were perfect, it wouldn't be.

Deja Vu All Over Again.

Okay you guys, pair up in threes!

We made too many wrong mistakes.

I'd give my right arm to be ambidextrous.

You wouldn't have won if we'd beaten you.

We're lost, but we're making good time.

It's tough to make predictions, especially about the future.

A nickel ain't worth a dime anymore.

I'm not going to buy my kids an encyclopedia. Let them walk to school like I did.

It's getting late early'

If you ask me anything I don't know, I'm not going to answer.

He must have made that before he died.

Even Napoleon had his Watergate.

If you can't imitate him, don't copy him.

No matter where you go, there you are.

You've got to be very careful if you don't know where you're going, because you might not get there.

I just want to thank everyone who made this day necessary.

If the fans don't wanna come out to the ballpark, no one can stop 'em.

It's not too far; it just seems like it is.

Pitching always beats batting — and vice-versa.

Ninety percent of all mental errors are in your head.

If I didn't wake up, I'd still be sleeping.

We made too many wrong mistakes.

We were overwhelming underdogs.

Bill Dickey is learning me his experience.

He hits from both sides of the plate. He's amphibious.

I always thought that record would stand until it was broken.

I didn't really say everything I said.

CHAPTER 4. BASKETBALL

I am often mentioned in the same sentence as Michael
Jordan. You know, 'That Scott Hastings, he's no Michael
Jordan'.
-Scott Hastings (1960 -)

To be successful you have to be selfish, or else you never
achieve. And once you get to your highest level, then you
have to be unselfish. Stay reachable. Stay in touch. Don't
isolate.
-Michael Jordan (1963 -)

We don't need referees in basketball, but it gives the white
guys something to do.
-Charles Barkley (1963 -)

The strength of the team is each individual member. The
strength of each member is the team.
-Phil Jackson (1945 -)

The first time I saw Dick Vitale, his hair was blowing in the
breeze. And he was too proud to chase it.
-Cliff Ellis (1945 -)

Ability may get you to the top, but it takes character to keep
you there.
-John Wooden (1910 – 2010)

Sometimes a player's greatest challenge is coming to grips
with his role on the team.
-Scottie Pippen (1965 -)

One man can be a crucial ingredient on a team, but one man cannot make a team.
-Kareem Abdul-Jabbar (1947 -)

But that's the thing about basketball: you don't play games on paper.
-Bill Simmons (1969 -)

Good thing in this business is that you just have to make one big shot and that's enough to make you forget 9 other shots that you missed.
-Guy Zucker

What is love? Love is playing every game like it's your last.
-Michael Jordan (1963 -)

I told him, 'Son what is it with you? Is it ignorance or apathy? He said 'Coach, I don't know and I don't care.'
-Frank Layden (1932 -)

I have missed more than 9000 shots in my career. I have lost almost 300 games. On 26 occasions I have been entrusted to take the game winning shot... and missed. And I have failed over and over and over again in my life. And that is why... I succeed.
-Michael Jordan (1963 -)

They've had so many injuries, they got to park their team bus in the handicapped zone.
-George Raveling (1937 -)

I never looked at the consequences of missing a big shot...
when you think about the consequences you always think of
a negative result.
-Michael Jordan (1963 -)

I love exercise. I could watch it all day.
-Bill Russell (1934 -)

Some people want it to happen, some wish it would happen,
others make it happen.
-Michael Jordan (1963 -)

I asked a referee if he would give me a technical foul for
thinking bad things about him. He said' Of course not.' I said,
'Well I think you stink.' And he gave me a technical foul. You
can't trust 'em.
-Jim Valvano (1946 – 93)

You never make any of the shots you never take. 87% of the
ones you do take, you'll miss too. I make 110% of my shots.
-Larry Bird (1956 -)

My responsibility is getting all my players playing for the
name on the front of the jersey, not the one on the back.
-Anon

Basketball doesn't build character it reveals it.
-Anon

Basketball is like photography, if you don't focus, all you
have is the negative.
-Dan Frisby

The idea is not to block every shot. The idea is to make your opponent believe that you might block every shot.
-Bill Russell (1934 -)

When the list of great coaches is finally read out, I believe Frank Layden will be there...listening.
-Pat Williams (1940 -)

If you are afraid of failure you don't deserve to be successful!
-Charles Barkley (1963 -)

You always have to give 100%, because if you don't someone, somewhere will give 100% and they will beat you when you meet.
-Ed Macauley (1928 – 2011)

You can't get much done in life if you only work on the days when you feel good.
-Jerry West (1938 -)

I'll do whatever it takes to win games, whether it's sitting on a bench waving a towel, handing a cup of water to a teammate, or hitting the game-winning shot.
-Kobe Bryant (1978 -)

Everything negative - pressure, challenges - are all an opportunity for me to rise.
-Kobe Bryant (1978 -)

Don't let what other people think decide who you are.
-Dennis Rodman (1961 -)

Me shooting 40% at the foul line is just God's way to say nobody's perfect.
-*Shaquille O'Neal (1972 -)*

Never mistake activity for achievement.
-*John Wooden (1910 – 2010)*

Everybody on a championship team doesn't get publicity, but everyone can say he's a champion.
-*Magic Johnson (1959 -)*

We try to stress the little things because little things lead to big things.
-*Steve Alford (1964 -)*

Practice to beat the best.
-*Dick Bennett (1943 -)*

If you want team play, you must stress defense. Defense makes players unselfish.
-*John Brady (1954 -)*

Criticize on defense and encourage on offense.
-*John Brady (1954 -)*

A guy who gives you less than what he has to give is, one, telling you what he thinks of you, and two, telling you what he thinks of himself.
-*Pete Carill (1930 -)*

I don't try to get players emotionally up for a game; it creates too many peaks and valleys... I strive for even keel; they will get up for the big games.
-*Denny Crum (1937 -)*

Systems win! Believe in your system, and then sell it to your players.
-*Billy Donovan (1965 -)*

A lot of late nights in the gym, a lot of early mornings, especially when your friends are going out, you're going to the gym, those are the sacrifices that you have to make if you want to be an NBA basketball player.
-*Jason Kidd (1973 -)*

Obstacles don't have to stop you. If you run into a wall, don't turn around and give up. Figure out how to climb it, go through it, or work around it.
-*Michael Jordan (1963 -)*

There is no such thing as a perfect basketball player, and I don't believe there is only one greatest player either.
-*Michael Jordan (1963 -)*

I'm not a role model... Just because I dunk a basketball doesn't mean I should raise your kids.
-*Charles Barkley (1963 -)*

I am sure that no man can derive more pleasure from money or power than I do from seeing a pair of basketball goals in some out of the way place.
-*James Naismith (1861 – 1939)*

Talent is God given. Be humble.
Fame is man-given. Be grateful.
Conceit is self-given. Be careful.
-*John Wooden (1910 – 2010)*

Basketball is a team game. But that doesn't mean all five players should have the same amount of shots.
-*Dean Edwards Smith (1931 – 2015)*

A basketball team is like the five fingers on your hand. If you can get them all together, you have a fist. That's how I want you to play.
-*Mike Krzyzewski (1947 -)*

You don't win championships by just being normal, by just being average.
-*William Theodore "Bill" Walton III (1952 -)*

Hard work beats talent when talent fails to work hard.
-*Kevin Wayne Durant (1988 -)*

Remember that basketball is a game of habits. If you make the other guy deviate from his habits, you've got him.
-*Bill Russell (1934 -)*

What distinguishes a great player is his presence. When he goes on to the court, his presence dominates the atmosphere.
-*Bill Russell (1934 -)*

You have a choice to make when you're not playing. Either you're invested and a great teammate, or you're not.
-*Brad Stevens (1976 -)*

What do you do with a mistake: recognize it, admit it, learn from it, forget it.
-*Dean Smith (1931 – 2015)*

Basketball is a beautiful game when the five players on the court play with one heartbeat.
-*Dean Smith (1931 – 2015)*

Do you want to choose winning over standing out? It's a choice every player on every championship team has to do.
-*Doc Rivers (1961 -)*

Good players want to be coached… Great players want to be told the truth.
-*Doc Rivers (1961 -)*

You can pick captains, but you can't pick leaders. Whoever controls the locker room controls the team.
-*Don Meyer (1944 – 2014)*

Practice shared suffering. If one guy messes up, everyone runs. If one guy does well, everyone benefits.
-*Don Meyer (1944 – 2014)*

Anytime you get an award as a coach, you've got to be the ultimate fool to think it wasn't your assistant coaches and all the players responsible for the award.
-*Don Meyer (1944 – 2014)*

Players with high character get better. Players with a serious approach get better. The fools never get better.
-Jeff Van Gundy (1962 -)

To go from where you are to where you want to be: you have to have a dream, a goal, and you have to be willing to work for it.
-Jim Valvano (1946 – 93)

Fans never fall asleep at our games, because they're afraid they might get hit by a pass.
-George Raveling (1937 -)

There are really only two plays: Romeo and Juliet, and put the darn ball in the basket.
-Abe Lemons (1922 – 2002)

Any time Detroit scores more than a hundred points and holds the other team below a hundred points, they almost always win.
-Doug Collins (1951 -)

Any American boy can be a basketball star if he grows up, up, up.
-Bill Vaughan (1915 – 77)

I'm in favour of drug tests, just so long as they are multiple choice.
-Kurt Rambis (1958 -)

In my prime I could have handled Michael Jordan. Of course, he would be only 12 years old.

-Jerry Sloan (1942 -)

CHAPTER 5. BOXING

Never fight ugly people - they have nothing to lose.
-Wayne Kelly (1919 – 2001)

All fighters are prostitutes and all promoters are pimps.
-Larry Holmes (1949-)

Boxing is just show business with blood.
-Frank Bruno (1961 -)

Rhythm is everything in boxing. Every move you make starts with your heart, and that's in rhythm or you're in trouble.
-Sugar Ray Robinson (1921 – 89)

If they can make penicillin out of mouldy bread, they can make something out of you.
-Muhammad Ali (1942 -)

I was a pretty good fighter. But it was the writers who made me great.
-Jack Dempsey (1895 – 1983)

Journalist Harry Cosell was going to be a boxer when he was a kid, only they couldn't find a mouthpiece big enough.
-Muhammad Ali (1942 -)

The tempt for greatness is the biggest drug in the world.
-Mike Tyson (1966 -)

You know why Mike Tyson's eyes water when he's having sex? Mace.
-Randall Cobb (1950-)

The fight is won or lost far away from witnesses—behind the lines, in the gym and out there on the road, long before I dance under those lights.
-Muhammad Ali (1942 -)

When I got up I stuck to my plan – stumbling forward and getting hit in the face.
-Randall Cobb (1950-)

Boxing is the toughest and loneliest sport in the world.
-Frank Bruno (1961 -)

I got into the ring with Muhammed Ali once and I had him worried for a while. He thought he had killed me.
-Tommy Cooper (1921 – 84)

In boxing you create a strategy to beat each new opponent, it's just like chess.
-Lennox Lewis (1965 -)

John Conteh had a neck built like a stately home staircase.
-Tom Davies (1972 -)

I hated every minute of training, but I said, 'Don't quit. Suffer now and live the rest of your life as a champion'.
-Muhammad Ali (1942 -)

I was once on a diet for two weeks running. All I lost was two weeks.
-*George Foreman (1949 -)*

A champion is someone who gets up when he can't.
-*Jack Dempsey (1895 – 1983)*

There's more to boxing than hitting. Not getting hit for instance.
-*George Foreman (1949 -)*

The man who has no imagination has no wings.
-*Muhammad Ali (1942 -)*

Me and Jakc LaMotta grew up in the same neighborhood. You wanna know how popular Jake was? When we played hide and seek, nobody ever looked for LaMotta
-*Rocky Graziano (1919 – 90)*

Boxing is a celebration of the lost religion of masculinity all the more trenchant for its being lost.
-*Joyce Carol Oates (1938 -)*

It's hard being black. Have you ever been black? I was black once – when I was poor.
-*Larry Holmes (1949 -)*

Only in America.
-*Don King (1931 -)*

When you can count your money you ain't got none.
-*Don King (1931 -)*

Don't count the days, make the days count.
-*Muhammad Ali (1942 -)*

Sadly America's oldest man has died at 114. However, Don King is confident that he will be able to find another opponent for George Foreman.
-*Bob Lacey (1953 -)*

To be a champ you have to believe in yourself when no one else will.
-*Sugar Ray Robinson (1921 – 89)*

They say money talks, but the only thing it ever said to me was goodbye.
-*Joe Louis (1914 – 81)*

To be a great champion you must first believe you are the best. If you're not, pretend you are.
-*Muhammad Ali (1942 -)*

Do I believe in superstitions? No. If you have superstitions it is bad luck.
-*Eric Lucas (1971 -)*

Boxers, like prostitutes, are in the business of ruining their bodies for the pleasure of strangers.
-*Wayne Kelly (1919 – 2001)*

In his prime Bugner had the body of a Greek statue, but he had far fewer moves.
-*Hugh McIlvanney (1934 -)*

Sure the fight was fixed. I fixed it with a right hand.

-George Foreman (1949-)

It's the repetition of affirmations that leads to belief. And once that belief becomes a deep conviction, things begin to happen.

-Muhammad Ali (1942 -)

To win takes a complete commitment of mind and body. When you can't make that commitment, they don't call you a champion anymore

Rocky Marciano (1923 – 69)

Hear about the Tyson computer? Two bytes and no memory.

-Phil Rosenthal (1960 -)

A champion shows who he is by what he does when he's tested. When a person gets up and says 'I can still do it', he's a champion.

-Evander Holyfield (1962 -)

The bell that tolls for all in boxing is the cash register.

-Bob Verdi (1968 -)

You don't think. It's all instinct. If you stop to think, you're gone.

-Sugar Ray Robinson (1921 – 89)

I'll beat him so bad he'll need a shoehorn to put his hat on.

-Muhammad Ali (1942 -)

It is not the size of a man but the size of his heart that matters.

-Evander Holyfield (1962 -)

It's hard to be humble, when you're as great as I am.

-Muhammad Ali (1942 -)

I'm scared every time I go into the ring, but it's how you handle it. What you have to do is plant your feet, bite down on your mouthpiece and say, 'Let's go.'

-Mike Tyson (1966 -)

Boxing is the ultimate challenge. There's nothing that can compare to testing yourself the way you do every time you step in the ring.

-Sugar Ray Leonard (1956 -)

When you saw me in the boxing ring fighting, it wasn't just so I could beat my opponent. My fighting had a purpose. I had to be successful in order to get people to listen to the things I had to say.

-Muhammad Ali (1942 -)

My power is discombobulatingly devastating. It's ludicrous these mortals even attempt to enter my realm.

-Mike Tyson (1966 -)

Now you see me, now you don't. George thinks he will, but I know he won't!

-Muhammad Ali (1942 -)

I'm so fast that last night I turned off the light switch in my hotel room and was in bed before the room was dark.
-*Muhammad Ali (1942 -)*

That's my gift. I let that negativity roll off me like water off a duck's back. If it's not positive, I didn't hear it. If you can overcome that, fights are easy.
-*George Foreman (1949-)*

Fighting, to me, seems barbaric. I don't really like it. I enjoy out-thinking another man and out-maneuvering him, but I still don't like to fight.
-*Sugar Ray Robinson (1921 – 89)*

A boxing match is like a cowboy movie. There's got to be good guys and there's got to be bad guys. And that's what people pay for - to see the bad guys get beat.
-*Sonny Liston (1932 – 70)*

I consider myself blessed. I consider you blessed. We've all been blessed with God-given talents. Mine just happens to be beating people up.
-*Sugar Ray Leonard (1956 -)*

The third man in the ring makes boxing possible.
-*Joyce Carol Oates (1938 -)*

Boxing is like jazz. The better it is, the less people appreciate it.
-*George Foreman (1949-)*

I'll be floating like a butterfly and stinging like a bee.
-*Muhammad Ali (1942 -)*

At home I am a nice guy: but I don't want the world to know. Humble people, I've found, don't get very far.
-Muhammad Ali (1942 -)

Boxing is the only sport you can get your brain shook, your money took and your name in the undertaker book.
-Joe Frazier (1944 – 2011)

Boxing was not something I truly enjoyed. Like a lot of things in life, when you put the gloves on, it's better to give than to receive.
-Sugar Ray Leonard (1956 -)

I am the astronaut of boxing. Joe Louis and Dempsey were just jet pilots. I'm in a world of my own.
-Muhammad Ali (1942 -)

A computer once beat me at chess, but it was no match for me at kick boxing.
-Emo Philips (1956 -)

Sonny Liston is nothing. The man can't talk. The man can't fight. The man needs talking lessons. The man needs boxing lessons. And since he's gonna fight me, he needs falling lessons.
-Muhammad Ali (1942 -)

I don't promote boxing, I promote people. Boxing is a catalyst to bring people together.
-Don King (1931 -)

Boxing is a lot of white men watching two black men beat each other up.
-Muhammad Ali (1942 -)

I've seen George Foreman shadow boxing, and the shadow won.
-Muhammad Ali (1942 -)

The hero and the coward both feel the same thing, but the hero uses his fear, projects it onto his opponent, while the coward runs. It's the same thing, fear, but it's what you do with it that matters.
-Cus D'Amato (1908 – 85)

The time may have come to say goodbye to Muhammad Ali, because very honestly, I don't think he can beat George Foreman.
-Howard Cosell (1918 – 95)

You can be free. You can be black. Look at me! I'm the Heavyweight Champion! Can't nobody stop me.
-Muhammad Ali (1942 -)

The three toughest fighters I ever fought were Sugar Ray Robinson, Sugar Ray Robinson and Sugar Ray Robinson. I fought Sugar so many times, I'm surprised I'm not diabetic.
-Jake LaMotta

I don't fight for legacy. I don't fight for none of that, I fight for that check. I'm in the check cashing business.
-Floyd Mayweather Jr. (1977 -)

Clay is so young and has been misled by the wrong people...
He might as well have joined the Ku Klux Klan.
-Floyd Patterson (1935 – 2006)

The possession of muscular strength and the courage to use
it in contests with other men for physical supremacy does
not necessarily imply a lack of appreciation for the finer and
better things of life.
-Jack Johnson (1975 -)

If you were surprised when Nixon resigned, just watch what
happens when I whup Foreman's behind!
-Muhammad Ali (1942 -)

When we started, it was based on lies. It's changing now.
There are no secrets in the business. You've got to come
with the truth, the whole truth and nothing but the truth. It's
becoming very confusing.
-Don King (1931 -)

I ain't got no quarrel with them Vietcong. They never called
me nigger.
-Muhammad Ali (1942 -)

It was a sucker punch. But you know who gets hit by sucker
punches? Suckers.
-Max Kellerman (1973 -)

Unlike any other sport, the objective in boxing is chillingly
simple: One man purposefully endeavors to inflict bodily
harm on another man.
-Howard Cosell (1918 – 95)

Sure there's been injuries and deaths in boxing but none of them serious.
-Alan Minter (1951 -)

Why waltz with a guy for 10 rounds if you can knock him out in one?
Rocky Marciano (1923 – 69)

To me, boxing is like a ballet, except there's no music, no choreography, and the dancers hit each other.
-Jack Handy (1949 -)

The dumbest question I was ever asked by a sportswriter was whether I hit harder with red or white gloves. As a matter of fact, I hit harder with red.
-Frank Crawford (1943 -)

If you even dream of beating me you'd better wake up and apologize.
-Muhammad Ali (1942 -)

My style is impetuous, my defense is impregnable, and I'm just ferocious, I want your heart, I want to eat his children.
-Mike Tyson (1966 -)

Lie down so I can recognise you.
-Willie Pep (1922 – 2006)

Chapter 6. Fishing

Fishing is the sport of drowning worms.
-Author Unknown

Fishing is a constant reminder of the democracy of life, of humility, and of human frailty. The forces of nature discriminate for no man.
-Herbert Hoover (1874 – 1964)

I go fishing not to find myself but to lose myself.
-Joseph Monniger (1953-)

There is no greater fan of fly fishing than the worm.
-Patrick F. McManus (1933 -)

Even a fish wouldn't get into trouble if it kept its mouth shut.
-Anon

Soon after I embraced the sport of angling I became convinced that I should never be able to enjoy it if I had to rely on the cooperation of the fish.
-Sparse Grey Hackle (1892 – 1983)

Anglers think they are divining some primeval natural force by outwitting a fish, a creature that never even got out of the evolutionary starting gate.
-Rich Hall (1954 -)

Many men go fishing all of their lives without knowing it is not fish they are after.
-Henry David Thoreau (1817 – 62)

A wild trout in its native habitat is a compact example of the Earth working well.
-Christopher Camuto

A bad day of fishing is better than a good day of work.
-Anon

Angling is extremely time consuming. That's sort of the whole point.
-Thomas McGuane (1939 -)

In every species of fish I've angled for, it is the ones that have got away that thrill me the most, the ones that keep fresh in my memory. So I say it is good to lose fish. If we didn't, much of the thrill of angling would be gone.
-Ray Bergman (1891 – 1967)

The best fisherman I know try not to make the same mistakes over and over again; instead they strive to make new and interesting mistakes and to remember what they learned from them.
-John Gierach (1946 -)

A trout is a moment of beauty known only to those who seek it.
-Arnold Gingrich(1903 – 76)

Time is but the stream I go a-fishing in.
-Henry David Thoreau (1817 – 62)

There are only two occasions when Americans respect privacy, especially in Presidents. Those are prayer and fishing.
-Herbert Hoover (1874 – 1964)

Fishing is a delusion entirely surrounded by liars in old clothes."
-Don Marquis (1878 – 1937)

All the romance of trout fishing exists in the mind of the angler and is in no way shared by the fish.
-Harold F. Blaisdell,

Everyone should believe in something; I believe I'll go fishing.
-Henry David Thoreau (1917 – 62)

The charm of fishing is that it is the pursuit of that which is elusive but attainable, a perpetual series of occasions for hope.
-John Buchan (1875 – 1940)

The fishing was good; it was the catching that was bad.
-A.K. Best

Even if you've been fishing for 3 hours and haven't gotten anything except poison ivy and sunburn, you're still better off than the worm.
-Anon

It has always been my private conviction that any man who pits his intelligence against a fish and loses has it coming.
-*John Steinbeck (1902 – 68)*

Fishing consists of a series of misadventures interspersed by occasional moments of glory.
-*Howard Marshall (1900 – 73)*

If fishing is a religion, fly fishing is high church.
-*Tom Brokaw (1940 -)*

What a tourist terms a plague of insects, the fly fisher calls a great hatch.
-*Patrick F. McManus (1933 -)*

Give a man a fish and he will eat for a day. Teach him how to fish and he will sit in a boat and drink beer all day.
-*Anon*

Some go to church and think about fishing, others go fishing and think about God.
-*Tony Blake*

Fishing is boring, unless you catch an actual fish, and then it is disgusting.
-*Dave Barry (1947 -)*

It matters not how many fish are in the sea - if you don't have any bait on your hook.
-*Dial West*

Don't stand by the water and long for fish; go home and weave a net.
-*Chinese proverb*

There he stands, draped in more equipment than a telephone lineman, trying to outwit an organism with a brain no bigger than a breadcrumb, and getting licked in the process.
-*Paul O'Neil*

In cross-examination, as in fishing, nothing is more ungainly than a fisherman pulled into the water by his catch.
- *Louis Nizer (1902 – 94)*

He liked fishing and seemed to take pride in being able to like such a stupid occupation.
— *Leo Tolstoy, Anna Karenina*

You do not cease to fish because you get old, You get old because you cease to fish!
-*Anon*

The finest gift you can give to any fisherman is to put a good fish back, and who knows if the fish that you caught isn't someone else's gift to you?
-*Lee Wulff (1905 – 91)*

I used to like fishing because I thought it had some larger significance. Now I like fishing because it's the one thing I can think of that probably doesn't.
-*John Gierach (1946 -)*

Fishing is a... discipline in the equality of men - for all men are equal before fish.
-Herbert Hoover (1874 – 1964)

If I fished only to capture fish, my fishing trips would have ended long ago.
-Zane Grey (1872 – 1939)

Writers fish for the right words like fishermen fish for, um, whatever those aquatic creatures with fins and gills are called.
-Jarod Kintz (1982 -)

Many of us probably would be better fishermen if we did not spend so much time watching and waiting for the world to become perfect.
-Norman Maclean (1902 – 90)

Fish are, of course, indispensable to the angler. They give him an excuse for fishing and justify the fly rod without which he would be a mere vagrant.
-Sparse Grey Hackle

Carpe Diem does not mean fish of the day.
-Anon

My biggest worry is that my wife (when I'm dead) will sell my fishing gear for what I said I paid for it.
-Koos Brandt

The fish and I were both stunned and disbelieving to find ourselves connected by a line.

-William Humphrey (1924 – 97)

No man ever steps in the same river twice, for it's not the same river and he's not the same man.

-Heraclitus (535 – 475BC)

I have fished through fishless days that I remember happily without regret.

-Roderick Haig-Brown (1908 – 77)

The man who coined the phrase "Money can't buy happiness", never bought himself a good fly rod!

-Reg Baird

Chapter 7. Golf

The older you get the stronger the wind gets...
-Jack Nicklaus (1940 -)

I'm the best. I just haven't played yet.
-Muhammad Ali (1942 -)

Golf appeals to the idiot in us and the child. Just how childlike golf players become is proven by their frequent inability to count past five.
-John Updike (1932 – 2009)

The game of golf is an enigma wrapped in a mystery impaled upon a conundrum.
-Peter Alliss (1931 -)

It is almost impossible to remember how tragic a place this world is when one is playing golf.
-Robert Lynd (1879 – 1949)

Golf is a game invented by the same people who think that music comes out of a bagpipe.
-Anon

Golf is so popular simply because it is the best game in the world at which to be bad.
-A.A. Milne (1882 – 1956)

Golf is a lot of walking broken up by disappointment and bad arithmetic.

-Anon

I have a tip that can take five strokes off anyone's golf game: it's called an eraser.

-Arnold Palmer (1929 -)

Golf is a game whose aim is to hit a very small ball into an even smaller hole, with weapons singularly ill designed for the purpose.

-Winston Churchill (1874 – 1965)

Golf is a game that is played on a five-inch course — the distance between your ears.

-Bobby Jones (1902 -71)

You know what they say about big hitters...the woods are full of them.

Jimmy Demeret (1910 – 83)

Golf is like a love affair. If you don't take it seriously, it's no fun; if you do take it seriously, it breaks your heart.

-Arthur Daley

Bob Hope has a beautiful short game. Unfortunately it is off the tee.

Jimmy Demeret (1910 – 83)

Golf is a fascinating game. It has taken me nearly forty years to discover that I can't play it.

-Ted Ray (1877 – 1943)

The only emotion Ben Hogan shows in defeat is surprise.
Jimmy Demeret (1910 – 83)

The number of shots taken by an opponent who is out of sight is equal to the square root of the sum of the number of curses heard plus the number of swishes.
-Michael Green (1927 -)

How has retirement affected my golf game? A lot more people beat me now.
-Dwight D. Eisenhower (1890 – 1969)

It's easy to see golf not as a game at all but as some whey-faced, nineteenth-century Presbyterian minister's fever dream of exorcism achieved through ritual and self-mortification.
-Bruce McCall (1935 -)

John Daly has the worst haircut I have ever seen in my life. It looks like he has a divot over each ear.
-David Feherty (1958 -)

Forget your opponents; always play against par.
-Sam Snead (1912 – 2002)

Jim Furyk has a swing like someone trying to kill a snake in a phone booth.
-David Feherty (1958 -)

If profanity had an influence on the flight of the ball, the game of golf would be played far better than it is.
-Horace G. Hutchinson (1859-1932)

I owe everything to golf. Where else could a guy with an IQ like mine make this much money.

-Hubert Green (1946 -)

They say golf is like life, but don't believe them. Golf is more complicated than that.

-Gardner Dickinson (1927 – 98)

Golf is a game where you yell fore, shoot six and write down five.

-Paul Harvey (1918 -2000)

Golf is a game to be played between cricket and death.

-Colin Ingleby-MacKenzie (1933 – 2006)

I guess there is nothing that will get your mind off everything like golf. I have never been depressed enough to take up the game, but they say you get so sore at yourself you forget to hate your enemies.

-Will Rogers (1879 – 1935)

A tricky short putt is a 'Dennis Wise' – a nasty five footer.

-Des Kelly (1965 -)

If a lot of people gripped a knife and fork the way they do a golf club, they'd starve to death.

-Sam Snead (1912 – 2002)

They say practice makes perfect. Of course it doesn't. For the vast majority of golfers it only consolidates imperfection.

-Henry Longhurst (1909 – 78)

Golf is a day spent in a round of strenuous idleness.
-William Wordsworth (1770 – 1850)

What other people may find in poetry or art museums, I find in the flight of a good drive.
-Arnold Palmer (1929 -)

Playing golf is like learning a foreign language.
-Henry Longhurst (1909 – 78)

The reason the pro tells you to keep your head down is so you can't see him laughing.
-Phyllis Diller (1919 – 2012)

The only sure rule in golf is, he who has the fastest cart never has to play the bad lie.
-Mickey Mantle (1931 – 95)

Golf combines two favorite American pastimes: taking long walks and hitting things with a stick.
-P.J. O'Rourke (1947 -)

Golf's three ugliest words: still your shot.
-Dave Marr (1933 – 97)

If you drink, don't drive. Don't even putt.
-Dean Martin (1917 – 95)

Watching Sam Snead practice hitting a golf ball is like watching a fish practice swimming.
-John Schlee (1939 – 2000)

Golf gives you an insight into human nature, your own as well as your opponent's.
-*Grantland Rice (1880 – 1954)*

They throw their clubs backwards, and that's wrong. You should always throw a club ahead of you so that you don't have to walk any extra distance to get it.
-*Tommy Bolt (1916 – 2008)*

There are two things that don't last – dogs who chase cars and professional golfers who putt for pars.
-*Lee Trevino (1939 -)*

Man blames fate for other accidents but feels personally responsible for a hole in one.
-*Martha Beckman*

When I die, bury me on the golf course so my husband will visit.
-*Anon*

I'm not saying my golf game went bad, but if I grew tomatoes, they'd come up sliced.
-*Miller Barber (1931 – 2013)*

If I can hit a curveball, why can't I hit a ball that is standing still on a course?
-*Larry Nelson (1947 -)*

If your opponent is playing several shots in vain attempts to extricate himself from a bunker, do not stand near him and audibly count his strokes. It would be justifiable homicide if

he wound up his pitiable exhibition by applying his niblick to your head.
-*Harry Vardon (1870 – 1937)*

They call it golf because all of the other four-letter words were taken.
-*Raymond Floyd (1942 -)*

Actually, the only time I ever took out a one-iron was to kill a tarantula. And it took a seven to do that.
-*Jim Murray (1919 – 98)*

The ardent golfer would play Mount Everest if somebody put a flagstick on top.
-*Pete Dye (1925 -)*

If you're caught on a golf course during a storm and are afraid of lightning, hold up a 1 iron. Not even God can hit a 1 iron.
Lee Trevino (1939 -)

Golf is played by twenty million mature American men whose wives think they are out having fun.
-*Jim Bishop (1907 – 87)*

I'm hitting the woods just great, but I'm having a terrible time getting out of them.
-*Harry Toscano (1942 -)*

I know I am getting better at golf because I'm hitting fewer spectators.
-*Gerald Ford (1913 – 2006)*

"Play it as it lies" is one of the fundamental dictates of golf. The other is "Wear it if it clashes."

-Henry Beard (1945 -)

I would like to deny all allegations by Bob Hope that during my last game of golf, I hit an eagle, a birdie, an elk and a moose.
-Gerald Ford (1913 – 2006)

The first time I played the Masters, I was so nervous I drank a bottle of rum before I teed off. I shot the happiest 83 of my life.
Chi Chi Rodriguez (1935 -)

My swing is so bad I look like a caveman killing his lunch.
-Lee Trevino (1939 -)

One of the most fascinating things about golf is how it reflects the cycle of life. No matter what you shoot — the next day you have to go back to the first tee and begin all over again and make yourself into something.
-Peter Jacobsen (1954 -)

Golf is a game in which you yell "fore," shoot six, and write down five.
-Paul Harvey (1918 – 2009)

Hockey is a sport for white men. Basketball is a sport for black men. Golf is a sport for white men dressed like black pimps.
Tiger Woods (1975 -)

A "gimme" can best be defined as an agreement between two golfers, neither of whom can putt very well.
–Anon

If I'm on the course and lightning starts, I get inside fast. If God wants to play through, let him.
-Bob Hope (1903 – 2003)

One minute you're bleeding. The next minute you're hemorrhaging. The next minute you're painting the Mona Lisa.
-Mac O'Grady (1951 -)

Go play golf. Go to the golf course. Hit the ball. Find the ball. Repeat until the ball is in the hole. Have fun. The end.
-Chuck Hogan (1969 -)

I was shooting in the low 70s and 60s by the time I was twelve. That's the great thing about golf. It doesn't matter how old or young you are; if you're 90 and can shoot a good score, people will want to play with you.
-Bubba Watson (1978 -)

To some golfers, the greatest handicap is the ability to add correctly.
-Anon

If you think it's hard to meet new people, try picking up the wrong golf ball.
-Jack Lemmon (1925 – 2001)

Golf is the closest game to the game we call life. You get bad breaks from good shots; you gct good breaks from bad shots - but you have to play the ball where it lies.
-Bobby Jones (1902 – 71)

A leading difficulty with the average player is that he totally misunderstands what is meant by concentration. He may think he is concentrating hard when he is merely worrying.
-Bobby Jones (1902 – 71)

Professional golf is the only sport where, if you win 20 percent of the time, you're the best.
-Jack Nicklaus (1940 -)

It takes hundreds of good golf shots to gain confidence, but only one bad one to lose it.
-Jack Nicklaus (1940 -)

Golf is deceptively simple and endlessly complicated; it satisfies the soul and frustrates the intellect. It is at the same time rewarding and maddening - and it is without a doubt the greatest game mankind has ever invented.
-Arnold Palmer (1929 -)

It's good sportsmanship to not pick up lost golf balls while they are still rolling.
-Mark Twain (1835 – 1910)

Although golf was originally restricted to wealthy, overweight Protestants, today it's open to anybody who owns hideous clothing.
-Dave Barry (1947 -)

I was a pitcher, and my dad played in college. The hardest day of my life was telling him I was going to quit to focus more on golf. But with golf, I felt like the game can't be perfected, and that motivated me.
-*Jordan Spieth (1993 -)*

Success in golf depends less on strength of body than upon strength of mind and character.
-*Arnold Palmer (1929 -)*

I learned one thing from jumping motorcycles that was of great value on the golf course, the putting green especially: Whatever you do, don't come up short.
-*Evel Knievel (1938 – 2007)*

You know, the Oscar I was awarded for The Untouchables is a wonderful thing, but I can honestly say that I'd rather have won the U.S. Open Golf Tournament.
-*Sean Connery (1930 -)*

Chapter 8. Horse Racing

Riding is the art of keeping a horse between yourself and the ground.
-Anon

The only decent people I ever saw at the racecourse were horses.
-James Joyce (1882 – 1941)

A racehorse is an animal that can take several thousand people for a ride at the same time.
-Anon

I would horsewhip you if I had a horse.
-Groucho Marx (1890 – 1977)

One way to stop a runaway horse is to bet on him.
-Jeffrey Barnard (1932 – 97)

There is nothing so good for the inside of a man as the outside of a horse.
-John Lubbock (1834 – 1913)

Bookmakers are pickpockets who allow you to use your own hands.
-WC Fields (1880 – 1946)

A difference of opinion is what makes horse racing and missionaries.
-Will Rogers (1879 – 1935)

You could remove the brains from 90 per cent of the jockeys and they would weigh the same.
-*John Francombe (1952 -)*

The race is not always to the swift, nor the battle to the strong, but that's the way to bet.
-*Damon Runyon (1880 – 1946)*

Lester Piggott has a face like a well-kept grave.
-*Jack Leach (1901 – 72)*

He was so learned that he could name a horse in nine languages; so ignorant that he bought a cow to ride on.
-*Benjamin Franklin (1706 – 90)*

If you remove the gambling, where is the fun in watching a load of horses being whipped by midgets?
-*Ian O'Doherty*

If a horse is no good, trade him for a dog, then shoot the dog.
-*Ben Jones (1941 -)*

John McCririck...looking like a hedge dragged through a man backwards.
-*Anon*

If an ass goes travelling, he'll not come back a horse.
-*Thomas Fuller (1608 – 61)*

I loathe Royal Ascot with a passion. All those people who wouldn't know which end bites trying to get spotted by Judith Chalmers, while you're trying to get the saddle down to the horse.
-Charles O'Brien

Half the failures in life arise from pulling in one's horse as he is leaping.
-Thomas Hood (1799 – 1845)

Horse sense is the thing a horse has which keeps it from betting on people.
-W.C. Fields (1880 – 1946)

A camel is a horse designed by committee.
-Alec Issigonis (1906 – 88)

The horse I bet on was so slow, the jockey kept a diary of the trip.
-Henny Youngman (1906 -88)

They say Princes learn no art truly, but the art of horsemanship. The reason is, the brave beast is no flatterer. He will throw a prince as soon as his groom.
-Ben Jonson (1572 – 1637)

You cannot train a horse with shouts and expect it to obey a whisper.
-Dagobert D. Runes (1902 – 82)

Ascot is so exclusive that it is the only racecourse in the world where the horses own the people.
-Art Buchwald (1925 – 2007)

If I were young, fast, healthy, and had a lot of money and my whole sex life ahead of me, I'd retire - like Secretariat.
-*Dick Butkus (1942 -)*

Owning a racehorse is probably the most expensive way of getting on to a racecourse for nothing.
-*Clement Freud (1924 – 2009)*

Paying alimony is like feeding hay to a dead horse.
-*Groucho Marx (1890 – 1977)*

A racehorse that consistently runs just a second faster than another horse is worth millions of dollars more. Be willing to give that extra effort that separates the winner from the one in second place.
H. Jackson Brown Jr (1940 -)

If you could call the thing a horse. If it hadn't shown a flash of speed in the straight, it would have got mixed up with the next race.
-*P. G. Wodehouse (1881 – 1975)*

It was the plainest Oaks field I have ever seen, and the paddock critic who expressed a decided preference for the horse of the policewoman on duty was no bad judge.
-*Roger Mortimer (1909 – 91)*

Secretariat is everything I am not. He is young, he has lots of hair, he is fast, he has a large bank account and his entire sex life is before him.
 -*Cy Burick Dayton*

You don't have to be Einstein to see that horse racing is dangerous. Those two ambulances driving behind you aren't there for the scenery.
-Tony McCoy (1974 -)

I have stood in a bar in Lambourn and been offered, in the space of five minutes, a poached salmon, a leg of a horse, a free trip to Chantilly, marriage, a large unsolicited loan, ten tips for a ten-horse race, two second-hand cars, a fight, and the copyright to a dying jockey's life story.
-Jeffrey Bernard (1932 – 97)

Take care to sell your horse before he dies. The art of life is passing losses on.
-Robert Frost (1874 – 1963)

A fence lasts three years, a dog lasts three fences, a horse lasts three dogs, and a man lasts three horses.
-German Proverb

If wishes were horses, there would be an easy explanation for all this horseshit.
-Anon

Riding: The art of keeping a horse between you and the ground.
-Anon

A loose horse is any horse sensible enough to get rid of its rider at an early stage and carry on unencumbered.
-Clive James (1939 -)

If you want to understand the effect of weight on a horse, try running for a bus with nothing in your hands. Then try doing it with your hands full of shopping. Then think about doing that for four and a half miles.

-Jenny Pitman (1946 -)

A real racehorse should have a head like a lady and the behind like a cook.

-Jack Leach (1901 – 72)

It is not enough for a man to know how to ride; he must know how to fall.

-Mexican Proverb

Horse racing is animated roulette.

-Roger Kahn (1927 -)

A good jockey doesn't need orders and a bad jockey couldn't carry them out anyway; so it's best not to give them any.

-Lester Piggott (1935 -)

No hour of life is wasted that is spent in the saddle.

-Winston Churchill (1874 – 1965)

Horses and jockeys mature earlier than people - which is why horses are admitted to racetracks at the age of two, and jockeys before they are old enough to shave.

-Dick Beddoes (1926 – 91)

A bookie is just a pickpocket who lets you use your own hands.

Henry Morgan

Any money I put on a horse is a sort of insurance policy to prevent it from winning.
-Frank Richardson (1916 – 2011)

Horses are uncomfortable in the middle and dangerous at both ends.
-Ian Fleming (1908 – 64)

I'm lucky because I have an athlete between my legs.
-Willie Carson (1942 -)

My horse was in the lead, coming down the home stretch, but the caddie fell off.
-Samuel Goldwyn (1879 – 1974)

There are, they say, fools, bloody fools and men who remount in a steeplechase.
-John Oaksey (1929 – 2012)

Love is. paying a £500 vet bill for a horse worth £50.
-Anon

Equestrian activity teaches young ladies to cope with large, friendly, but dumb creatures – the ideal training for marriage.
-Anon

Brigadier Gerard did not win the Derby because he did not run in it. He did not run in it because he was not bred for it. He wasn't bred for it because I couldn't afford it.
-John Hislop (1911 - 94)

The 1980 Grand National - a tremendous race, with four finishers out of 30 starters, so that by the end there were far more BBC commentators than horses.
-*Clive James (1939 -)*

I am not one of the people who believe that the main reason why a chap becomes a bookmaker is because he is too scared to steal and too heavy to become a jockey.
-*Noel Whitcombe (1918 – 93)*

A lovely horse is always an experience.... It is an emotional experience of the kind that is spoiled by words.
-*Beryl Markham (1902 – 86)*

In betting on races, there are two elements that are never lacking - hope as hope, and an incomplete recollection of the past.
-*Edward V. Lucas (1868 – 1938)*

In most betting shops you will see three windows marked 'Bet Here', but only one window with the legend 'Pay Out".
-*Jeffrey Bernard (1932 – 97)*

A horse is the projection of peoples' dreams about themselves - strong, powerful, beautiful - and it has the capability of giving us escape from our mundane existence.
-*Pam Brown (1948 -)*

If your horse says no, you either asked the wrong question, or asked the question wrong.
- *Pat Parelli (1954 -)*

No one has ever bet enough on a winning horse.
-*Richard Sasuly (1913 -)*

A horse never runs so fast as when he has other horses to catch up and outpace.
-*Ovid (43BC – 18AD)*

Remember, Lady Godiva put all she had on a horse and she lost her shirt!
-*W. C. Fields (1880 – 1946)*

The horse I bet on had four legs and flies - unfortunately it was a dead horse.
-*Anon*

The only exercise I get is walking to the betting office.
-*Peter O'Sullevan (1918 – 2015)*

Horses are red,
Horses are blue,
Horses that lose
Are turned into glue.
-*Anon*

All horses deserve, at least once in their lives, to be loved by a little girl.
-*Anon*

CHAPTER 9. ICE HOCKEY

Give blood. Play hockey.
-Anon

Hockey belongs to the Cartoon Network, where a person can be pancaked by an ACME anvil, then expanded - accordion-style - back to full stature, without any lasting side effect.
-Steve Rushin (1966 -)

Hockey captures the essence of Canadian experience in the New World. In a land so inescapably and inhospitably cold, hockey is the chance of life, and an affirmation that despite the deathly chill of winter we are alive.
-Stephen Leacock (1869 – 1944)

By the age of 18, the average American has witnessed 200,000 acts of violence on television, most of them occurring during Game 1 of the NHL playoff series.
-Steve Rushin (1966 -)

A puck is a hard rubber disc that hockey players strike when they can't hit one another.
-Jimmy Cannon (1909 – 1973)

How would you like a job where, every time you make a mistake, a big red light goes on and 18,000 people boo?
-Jacques Plante (1929 – 86)

Some people skate to the puck. I skate to where the puck is going to be.
-Wayne Gretzky (1961 -)

Ice hockey players can walk on water.
-Anon

Street hockey is great for kids. It's energetic, competitive, and skillful. And best of all it keeps them off the street.
-Anon

Hockey players wear numbers because you can't always identify the body with dental records.
-Anon

High sticking, tripping, slashing, spearing, charging, hooking, fighting, unsportsmanlike conduct, interference, roughing... everything else is just figure skating.
-Anon

When Hell freezes over, I'll play hockey there too.
-Anon

I went to a fight the other night and a hockey game broke out.
-Rodney Dangerfield (1921 – 2004)

Some guys play hockey. Gretzky plays 40 mph chess.
-Lowell Cohn

Is that a beard, or is Niedermayer eating a muskrat?
-Harry Neale (1937 -)

You'll always miss 100% of the shots you don't take.
-Wayne Gretzky (1961 -)

Half the game is mental; the other half is being mental.
-Jim McKenny

Hockey is murder on ice.
-Jim Murray (1946 -)

Nobody's a natural. You work hard to get good and then work to get better. It's hard to stay on top.
-Paul Coffey (1961 -)

We get nose jobs all the time in the NHL, and we don't even have to go to the hospital.
-Brad Park (1948 -)

We take the shortest route to the puck and arrive in ill humor.
-Bobby Clarke (1949 -)

I'm not dumb enough to be a goalie.
-Brad Hull (1979 -)

The goal is too small and the goalies are too big.
-Scotty Bowman (1933 -)

October is not only a beautiful month but marks the precious yet fleeting overlap of hockey, baseball, basketball, and football.
-Jason Love (1987 -)

Four out of five dentists surveyed recommended playing hockey.
-Anon

A fast body-contact game played by men with clubs in their hands and knives laced to their feet.
-Paul Gallico (1897 – 1976)

Our first priority was staying alive. Our second was stopping the puck.
-Glenn Hall (1931 -)

The three important elements of hockey are: forecheck, backcheck and paycheck.
-Gil Perreault (1950 -)

Hockey is a man's game. The team with the most real men wins.
-Brian Burke (1955 -)

The only way you can check Gretzky is to hit him when he is standing still singing the national anthem.
-Harry Sinden (1932 -)

All hockey players are bilingual. They know English and profanity.
- Gordie Howe (1928 -)

Ice hockey is a form of disorderly conduct in which the score is kept.
-Doug Larson (1926 -)

Every day you guys look worse and worse, and today you played like tomorrow.
-John Mariucci (1916 – 87)

Playing goal is like being shot at.
-Jacques Plante (1929 – 86)

Red ice sells hockey tickets.
-Bob Stewart (1950 -)

Hockey's the only place where a guy can go nowadays and watch two white guys fight.
-Frank Deford (1938 -)

Hockey is the original extreme sport.
-Tom Ward (1971 -)

Hockey is figure skating in a war zone.
-Anon

Goals live on the other side of obstacles and challenges. Be relentless in pursuit of those goals, especially in the face of obstacles. Along the way, make no excuses and place no blame.
-Ray Bourque (1960 -)

CHAPTER 10. RUGBY

Rugby is a good occasion for keeping thirty bullies far from the center of the city.
-Oscar Wilde (1854 – 1900)

Rugby is a game for big buggers. If you're not a big bugger, you get hurt. I wasn't a big bugger but I was a fast bugger and therefore I avoided the big buggers.
-Spike Milligan (1918 – 2002)

Rugby is a wonderful show: dance, opera and, suddenly, the blood of a killing.
-Richard Burton (1925 – 84)

The tactical difference between Association Football and Rugby with its varieties seems to be that in the former, the ball is the missile, in the latter, men are the missiles. *-Alfred E. Crawley (1867 – 1924)*

Rugby is great. The players don't wear helmets or padding; they just beat the living daylights out of each other and then go for a beer. I love that.
-Joe Theismann (1949 -)

Good big blokes are better than good little blokes. Then again, good little blokes are better than dud big blokes. And dud big blokes should play something other than Rugby.
-Bob Dwyer (1940 -)

Ballroom dancing is a contact sport. Rugby is a collision sport.
-Heyneke Meyer (1967 -)

I'm still an amateur, of course, but I became rugby's first millionaire five years ago.
David Campese (1962 -)

I prefer rugby to soccer. I enjoy the violence in rugby, except when they start biting each other's ears off.
-Elizabeth Taylor (1932 – 2011)

I like to think I play rugby as it should be played - there are no yellow or red cards in my collection - but I cannot say I'm an angel.
-Jonny Wilkinson (1979-)

The advantage law is the best law in rugby, because it lets you ignore all the others for the good of the game.
-Derek Robinson (1932 -)

I've always said that playing rugby in Spain is like being a bullfighter in Japan.
-Javier Bardem (1969 -)

The Holy Writ of Gloucester Rugby Club demands: first, that the forwards shall win the ball; second, that the forwards shall keep the ball; and third, the backs shall buy the beer.
-Doug Ibbotson

If I had been a winger, I might have been daydreaming and thinking about how to keep my kit clean for next week.
-Bill Beaumont (1952 -)

I'm a huge Rugby Union fan, which is a bit like American football - but tougher.
-*Alexander Hanson (1961 -)*

A major rugby tour by the British Isles to New Zealand is a cross between a medieval crusade and a prep school outing.
-*John Hopkins*

Nobody in Rugby should be called a genius. A genius is a guy like Norman Einstein.
-*Jono Gibbes (1977 -)*

I don't know why prop forwards play rugby.
-*Lionel Weston (1947 -)*

I was absolutely a non-starter at games. My report for rugby said, 'Nigel's chief contribution is his presence on the field.' I used to pray for rain and sometimes it did rain - and we played anyway.
-*Nigel Rees (1944 -)*

A forward's usefulness to his side varies as to the square of his distance from the ball.
-*Clarrie Gibbons*

Beer and Rugby are more or less synonymous.
-*Chris Laidlaw (1943 -)*

League is much, much more physical than Union, and that's before anyone starts breaking the rules.
-*Adrian Hadley (1963 -)*

Rugby may have many problems, but the gravest is undoubtedly that of the persistence of summer.
-*Chris Laidlaw (1943 -)*

Me? As England's answer to Jonah Lomu? Joanna Lumley, more likely.
-*Damian Hopley (1970 -)*

The French are predictably unpredictable.
-*Andrew Mehrtens (1973 -)*

In my time, I've had my knee out, broken my collarbone, had my nose smashed, a rib broken, lost a few teeth, and ricked my back; but as soon as I get a bit of bad luck I'm going to quit the game.
-*J. W. Robinson*

If the game is run properly as a professional game, you do not need 57 old farts running rugby.
-*Will Carling (1965 -)*

The women sit, getting colder and colder, on a seat getting harder and harder, watching oafs, getting muddier and muddier.
-*Virginia Graham (1912 – 98)*

The only trophy we won this day, was the blood and sweat we left on the pitch…. and it was enough.
–Anon

Don't ask me about emotions in the Welsh dressing room. I'm someone who cries when he watches Little House on the Prairie.
-*Robert Norster (1957 -)*

Forwards are the gnarled and scarred creatures who have a propensity for running into and bleeding all over each other.
-Peter Fitzsimmons (1961 -)

England's coach Jack Rowell, an immensely successful businessman, has the acerbic wit of Dorothy Parker and, according to most New Zealanders, a similar knowledge of rugby.
-Mark Reason (1966 -)

It doesn't matter whether it's cricket, rugby union, rugby league - we all hate England.
-John O'Neill (1951 -)

If you can't take a punch, you should play table tennis.
-Pierre Berbizier (1958 -)

Sort of desolate, decayed, the smell of - I don't want to dramatise it - but death, you know. That is what it feels like, no-man's-land, and it is not a nice place to be.
-Anton Oliver (1975 -)

No leadership, no ideas. Not even enough imagination to thump someone in the line-up when the ref wasn't looking.
-J.P.R. Williams (1949 -)

The relationship between the Welsh and the English is based on trust and understanding. They don't trust us and we don't understand them.
-Dudley Wood (1930 -)

We've lost seven of our last eight matches. Only team that we've beaten was Western Samoa. Good job we didn't play the whole of Samoa.
-Gareth Davies (1955 -)

Remember that rugby is a team game; all 14 of you make sure you pass the ball to Jonah.
-Anon fax to N.Z. team (1995)

Colin Meads is the kind of player you expect to see emerging from a ruck with the remains of a jockstrap between his teeth.
-Tom O'Reilly

In 1823, William Webb Ellis first picked up the ball in his arms and ran with it. And for the next 156 years forwards have been trying to work out why.
-Sir Tasker Watkins (1918 - 2007)

Rugby backs can be identified because they generally have clean jerseys and identifiable partings in their hair... come the revolution the backs will be the first to be lined up against the wall and shot for living parasitically off the work of others.
-Peter Fitzsimmons (1961 -)

I think you enjoy the game more if you don't know the rules. Anyway, you're on the same wavelength as the referees.
-Jonathan Davies (1962 -)

Rugby is played by men with odd shaped balls.
-Anon

You've got to get your first tackle in early, even if it's late.
-Ray Gravell (1951 – 2007)

I'd like to thank the press from the heart of my bottom.
-Nick Easter (1978 -)

He scored that try after only 22 seconds – totally against the run of play.
-*Murray Mexted (1953 -)*

Sure there have been injuries and deaths in rugby – but none of them serious.
-*Doc Mayhew (1955 -)*

I never comment on referees and I'm not going to break the habit of a lifetime for that prat.
-*Ewan McKenzie (1965 -)*

Well, either side could win it, or it could be a draw.
-*Murray Mexted (1953 -)*

Strangely, in slow motion replay, the ball seemed to hang in the air for even longer.
-*Murray Mexted (1953 -)*

Rugby football is a game I can't claim absolutely to understand in all its niceties, if you know what I mean. I can follow the broad, general principles, of course. I mean to say, I know that the main scheme is to work the ball down the field somehow and deposit it over the line at the other end and that, in order to squalch this programme, each side is allowed to put in a certain amount of assault and battery and do things to its fellow man which, if done elsewhere, would result in 14 days without the option, coupled with some strong remarks from the Bench.
-*P. G. Wodehouse (1881 – 1975)*

CHAPTER 11. SOCCER

Some people tell me that we professional players are soccer slaves. Well, if this is slavery, give me a life sentence.
-Sir Bobby Charlton (1937 -)

Football is the ballet of the masses.
-Dmitri Shostakovich (1906 – 75)

In his life, a man can change wives, political parties or religions but he cannot change his favorite soccer team.
-Eduardo Hughes Galeano (1940 – 2015)

I don't believe skill was, or ever will be, the result of coaches. It is a result of a love affair between the child and the ball.
-Roy Keane (1971 -)

To say that these men paid their shillings to watch twenty-two hirelings kick a ball is merely to say that a violin is wood and catgut, and that Hamlet is so much paper and ink.
-J.B. Priestley (1894 – 1984)

The ball is round, the game lasts ninety minutes, and everything else is just theory.
-Josef "Sepp" Herberger (1897 – 1977)

International football is the continuation of war by other means.
-George Orwell (1903 – 50)

In football everything is complicated by the presence of the opposite team.
-*Jean-Paul Sartre (1905 – 80)*

I know more about soccer than about politics.
-*Harold Wilson (1916 – 85)*

At a football club, there's a holy trinity - the players, the manager and the supporters. Directors don't come into it. They are only there to sign the cheques.
-*Bill Shankly (1913 – 81)*

The rules of soccer are very simple, basically it is this: if it moves, kick it. If it doesn't move, kick it until it does.
-*Phil Woosnam (1932 – 2013)*

Success is no accident. It is hard work, perseverance, learning, studying, sacrifice and most of all, love of what you are doing or learning to do.
-*Pele (1940 -)*

Whoever invented soccer should be worshipped as god.
-*Hugo Sánchez (1958 -)*

Football is a simple game; 22 men chase a ball for 90 minutes and at the end, the Germans win.
-*Gary Lineker (1960 -)*

We must have had 99 percent of the game. It was the other three percent that cost us the match.
-*Ruud Gullit (1962 -)*

I have the chance to do for a living what I like the most in life, and that's playing football. I can make people happy and enjoy myself at the same time.

-Ronaldinho (1980 -)

Life is like a game of soccer. You need goals. If there are no goals in your life then you can't win.

-Anon

Soccer is not just about scoring goals. It's about winning.

-Anon

Give a man a soccer ball, he plays for a moment. Teach a man to play soccer, he plays for a life time.

-Anon

To me, soccer is so much more than a ball and two goals; it connects people from all of the corners of the world.

-Anon

Why is there only one ball for 22 players? If you gave a ball to each of them, they'd stop fighting for it.

-Anon

I like tricks; I like to dazzle. Dribbling and leaving your opponent on his backside is what life is for. If I achieve what I want to, then I'll mark a distinct era in football. I'm the Che Guevara of modern soccer.

-Sergio Aguero (1988 -)

I'm attracted to soccer's capacity for beauty. When well played, the game is a dance with a ball.
- *Eduardo Hughes Galeano (1940 – 2015)*

When I was ten, I wrote an essay on what I would be when I grew up and said I would be a professional soccer player and a comedian in off season.
-Will Ferrell

Soccer is a matter of life and death, except more important.
-Bill Shankly

I wouldn't say I was the best manager in the business. But I was in the top one.
-Brian Clough (1935 – 2004)

They say Rome wasn't built in a day, but I wasn't on that particular job.
-Brian Clough (1935 – 2004)

Players lose you games, not tactics. There's so much crap talked about tactics by people who barely know how to -win at dominoes.
-Brian Clough (1935 – 2004)

For Tony Adams to admit he's an alcoholic took an awful lot of bottle.
-Ian Wright (1963 -)

The River Trent is lovely, I know because I have walked on it for 18 years
-Brian Clough (1935 – 2004)

It's a huge honour to wear No 7 at Liverpool. I think about the legends: Dalglish, Keegan and that Australian guy.
-Luis Suarez (1987 -)

We talk about it for 20 minutes and then we decide I was right
-Brian Clough (1935 – 2004)

Pastore wouldn't get a beach ball off me if we were locked in a phone box. He's turd. Anyone who thinks he isn't is clueless.
-Joey Barton (1982 -)

Good managers make good sides. There's no such thing as a side making a manager
-Brian Clough (1935 – 2004)

I'd have given my right arm to be a pianist.
-Bobby Robson (1933 – 2009)

Beckham? His wife can't sing and his barber can't cut hair.
-Brian Clough (1935 – 2004)

I hope I don't come across as bitter and twisted, but that man (Mick McCarthy) can rot in hell for all I care.
-Roy Keane (1971 -)

They didn't want an England manager who was prepared to call the Italians cheating bastards
-Brian Clough (1935 – 2004)

I knew it wasn't going to be our day when I arrived at Links Park and found that we had a woman running the line. She should be at home making the tea or the dinner for her man who comes in after he has been to the football.
-Peter Hetherston (1964 -)

We didn't underestimate them. They were a lot better than we thought.
-Bobby Robson (1933 – 2009)

I regret telling the entire world and his dog how good a manager I was. I knew I was the best but I should have said nowt and kept the pressure off 'cos they'd have worked it out for themselves.
-Brian Clough (1935 – 2004)

Mind you, I've been here during the bad times too - one year we came second
-Bob Paisley (1919 – 96)

Ah yes, Frank Sinatra. He met me once y'know?
-Brian Clough (1935 – 2004)

Every dog has its day - and today is woof day! Today I just want to bark.
-Ian Holloway (1963 -)

When I go, God's going to have to give up his favourite chair.
-Brian Clough (1935 – 2004)

There is no pressure when you are making a dream come true.
-Neymar Santos (1992 -)

Without being too harsh on David, he cost us the match.
-Ian Wright (1963 -)

A lot of football success is in the mind. You must believe you are the best and then make sure that you are.
-Bill Shankly (1913 – 81)

Not to win is guttering.
-Mark Noble (1987 -)

The trouble with referees is that they know the rules, but they do not know the game.
-Bill Shankly (1913 – 81)

I don't like losing but I've mellowed. I maybe have a short fuse but it goes away quicker now.
-Alex Ferguson (1941 -)

Some people think football is a matter of life and death. I don't like that attitude. I can assure them it is much more serious than that.
-Bill Shankly (1913 – 81)

In football, the worst blindness is only seeing the ball.
-Nelson Falcão Rodrigues (1912 – 80)

Aim for the sky and you'll reach the ceiling. Aim for the ceiling and you'll stay on the floor.
-Bill Shankly (1913 – 81)

The person that said winning isn't everything, never won anything.
-Mia Hamm (1972 -)

Of course I didn't take my wife to see Rochdale as an anniversary present. It was her birthday. Would I have got married in the football season? Anyway, it was Rochdale reserves.
-Bill Shankly (1913 – 81)

Fail to prepare, prepare to fail." – Roy Keane
If Everton were playing at the bottom of the garden, I'd pull the curtains
-Bill Shankly (1913 – 81)

I know this is a sad occasion but I think that Dixie would be amazed to know that even in death he could draw a bigger crowd than Everton can on a Saturday Afternoon.
-Bill Shankly (1913 – 81)

It is better to win ten times 1-0 than to win once 10-0.
-Vahid Halilhodžic (1952 -)

If you are first you are first. If you are second, you are nothing
-Bill Shankly (1913 – 81)

Football is war minus the shooting.
-George Orwell (1903 – 50)

Chapter 12 Tennis

In tennis you're on an island. Of all the games men and women play, tennis is the closest to solitary confinement.
–Andre Agassi (1970 -)

Dreams do come true if you keep believing in yourself. Anything is possible.
–Jennifer Capriati (1976 -)

Victory is fleeting. Losing is forever.
-Billie Jean King (1943 -)

If you can keep playing tennis when somebody is shooting a gun down the street, that's concentration. I didn't grow up playing at the country club.
-Serena Williams

Everybody loves success but they hate successful people.
-John McEneroe (1959 -)

If you don't love to run, please take up golf.
-Rick Macci

To err is human. To put the blame on someone else is doubles.
-Anon

Speed in tennis is a strange mixture of intuition, guesswork, footwork and hair-trigger reflexes. Many of the players famed for quickness on court would finish dead last in a field of schoolgirls in a race over any distance more than ten yards.
-Eugene Scott (1945 -)

A champion is afraid of losing. Everyone else is afraid of winning.
-Billie Jean King (1943 -)

Love is nothing in tennis but everything in life.
-Anon

The ideal attitude is to be physically fit and mentally loose.
-Arthur Ashe (1943 – 93)

I just try to play tennis and don't find excuses. You know, I just lost because I lost, not because my arm was sore.
-Goran Ivanisevic (1971 -)

Conversation is like playing Tennis with a ball made of Krazy Putty that keeps coming back over the net in a different shape.
-David Lodge (1935 -)

In sports, you simply aren't considered a real champion until you have defended your title successfully. Winning it once can be a fluke; winning it twice proves you are the best.
-Althea Gibson (1927 – 2003)

I love the winning, I can take the losing, but most of all I love to play.
-Boris Becker (1967 -)

Experience is a great advantage. The problem is when you get the experience you are too damned old to do anything about it.
-Jimmy Connors (1952 -)

True heroism is remarkably sober, very undramatic. It is not the urge to surpass all others at whatever cost, but the urge to serve others at whatever cost.
-Arthur Ashe (1943 – 93)

The serve was invented so the net could play.
-Bill Cosby (1937 -)

I never knew I was grunting, it was just part of my strokes.
-Monica Seles (1973 -)

I play each point like my life depends on it.
-Rafael Nadal (1986 -)

Tennis is a perfect combination of violent action taking place in an atmosphere of total tranquility.
-Billie Jean King (1943 -)

Tennis is mostly mental. You win or lose the match before you even go out there.
-Venus Williams (1980 -)

Tennis uses the language of life. Advantage, service, fault, break, love — the basic elements of tennis are those of everyday existence, because every match is a life in miniature.
-*Andre Agassi (1970 -)*

The depressing thing about tennis is that no matter how good I get, I'll never be as good as a wall.
-*Mitch Hedberg (1968 – 2005)*

The fifth set is not about tennis, it's about nerves.
-*Boris Becker (1967 -)*

The mark of great sportsmen is not how good they are at their best, but how good they are at their worst
–*Martina Navratilova (1956 -)*

Most tennis players greatly overestimate what they can achieve over a short time, and greatly underestimate what they can do over a long time. So keep plugging away, and when you look back, you'll be amazed.
-*Neil Witherow*

You don't have to be pretty for people to come and see you play. At the same time, if you're a good athlete, it doesn't mean you're not a woman.
–*Martina Navratilova (1956 -)*

You'll hear a lot of applause in your life, but none will mean more to you than that applause from your peers. I hope each of you hears that at the end.
– *Andre Agassi (1970 -)*

Tennis belongs to the individualistic past - a hero, or at most a pair of friends or lovers, against the world.
-Jacques Barzun (1907 – 2012)

Behind every tennis player, there is another tennis player.
-John McPhee (1931 -)

I have always considered tennis as a combat in an arena between two gladiators who have their racquets and their courage as their weapons.
-Yannick Noah (1960 -)

Ladies, here's a hint. If you're up against a girl with big boobs, bring her to the net and make her hit backhand volleys. That's the hardest shot for the well-endowed.
-Billie Jean King (1943 -)

Good shot, bad luck, and hell are the five basic words to be used in a game of tennis, though these, of course, can be slightly amplified.
-Virginia Graham (1912 – 98)

When I was 40, my doctor advised me that a man in his 40s shouldn't play tennis. I heeded his advice carefully and could hardly wait until I reached 50 to start again.
-Hugo L. Black (1886 – 1971)

In tennis the addict moves about a hard rectangle and seeks to ambush a fuzzy ball with a modified snow-shoe.
-Elliot Chaze (1915 – 90)

It's one-on-one out there, man. There ain't no hiding. I can't pass the ball.
-*Pete Sampras (1971 -)*

New Yorkers love it when you spill your guts out there. Spill your guts at Wimbledon and they make you stop and clean it up.
-*Jimmy Connors (1952 -)*

One day you can be a kid, but another day you have to be like this is your job, you play tennis. You have to work for that.
-*Martina Hingis (1980 -)*

When I play, I feel like in a theatre, why should I look ugly then, because I'm a tennis player?
-*Anna Kournikova (1981 -)*

The difference between involvement and commitment is like ham and eggs. The chicken is involved; the pig is committed.
–*Martina Navratilova (1956 -)*

As a tennis player you can win and you can lose, and you have to be ready for both. I practised self-control as a kid. But as you get older they both - winning and losing - get easier.
–*Rafael Nadal (1986 -)*

Tennis: the most perfect combination of athleticism, artistry, power, style, and wit. A beautiful game, but one so remorselessly travestied by the passage of time.
-*Martin Amis (1949 -)*

Start where you are. Use what you have. Do what you can.
-*Arthur Ashe (1943 – 93)*

This [defeat] has taught me a lesson, but I'm not sure what it is.
–*John McEnroe (1959 -)*

My theory is that if you buy an ice-cream cone and make it hit your mouth, you can play [tennis]. If you stick it on your forehead, your chances are less.
-*Vic Braden (1929 – 2014)*

ONE LAST THING...

If you enjoyed this book or found it useful I'd be very grateful if you'd post a short review on Amazon. Your support really does make a difference and I read all the reviews personally so I can get your feedback and make this book even better.

If you'd like to leave a review then all you need to do is click the review link on this book's page on Amazon.

There are also other books by the author;

The Big Book of Quotes

501 Quotes about Love

501 Quotes about Life

Many thanks for your support

Made in the USA
Columbia, SC
09 October 2022

69203817R00072